Muses & Vices

Antione Denzel Lacey

"Don't dwell in the ambience of the stationary because the environment is soon to be changed."

- Antione Denzel Lacey

CONTENTS

Muses & Vices

DEDICATION

This book is a poetic dedication to God and my mother. In the midst of my darkness, they've always seen the light within me. It has been times I distanced myself away from my reflection and they've reminded me that I'm their brightest star even in a cluster of confusion. Also this book is dedicated to anyone who believer in their dreams, God can open any door – even if the knobs are broken!

Today

Today,
I embraced the sunlight
And put my darkness behind me.
I rejuvenated
My soul with the lull chimes of my temple.

Today,
I stepped out the shadows of configuration,
Shedding my depressive exoskeleton
And realized who I am.
This is me,
A metamorphosing man of peace.

Today,
I feel…
Free.
I feel happy.
The padded white walls of my anxiety,
Won't constrain me no more.

I live with the aspirations
Of today,
Not fearing tomorrow.

Because today,

I live with *no regrets*.

Today,

I am alive.

This body isn't a horrible mirage,

And this soul says I am here.

I am whole.

Self

My pride can be the silence of the tongue,

Or the loud speaker of a siren.

I am prideful.

Prideful enough to ignore the outside voices

Telling me right,

When I know it's wrong.

I dare not to utter the repetition

Of ignorance.

Many don't see my vision,

Nor will they sit in the throne of my kingdom.

I won't ask for help,

Unless I'm neck deep in the high water

Of poverty

Or drowning in the horrifying depths

Of my thoughts.

My trust,

Is the epitome of being cautious

At a yellow light.

I've had a fall off with God.

My faith became as blind as the foes

Who used his name as leverage.

Their whispers,

Became the serpents in my ears,

Separating me from divine truth.

Now,

My happiness is in my favor.

I've learned to walk in the light

And control my faith.

I have chronophobia.

This fear exists because of time.

Time isn't promised to a black boy

From the slums.

It's only taken away by nameless bullets.

If it can only be stationary,

I would bask in the memories

Of my mother's love.

I'm immortalized to pain.

I wear my heart

On my sleeve so much,

Every blood stain becomes a story.

These stories reminisce
On the darkest hours in my life.
I tried to use bleach,
But this heart would tarnish
In the wash.

My favorite bird is a crow.
Mysterious creature of the sky.
By nature,
It is misunderstood
Like I am.

Given the judgement
Of evil,
By the color of its feathers.
Like the pigment
Of my skin,
Judgement is placed upon it.

The ways of the world
Are immortal.
With these words,
It shall live on forever.

Antione Denzel Lacey

Momma

Twenty-four is the luck number
Being bosomed in momma's grace.
Her love is the warm blanket
Cradling me until my nightmares
Are blissful dreams.

My momma is my guardian angel.
By the Excalibur of her words,
She'll smite down anyone
Who threatens my composer.

Hardships were the winds,
Momma was the house of protection.
She protected me in her ambiance,
Made me realize what humbleness meant.

Choosing between poverty and happiness,
We chose to stay happy.
We devoured the cold meals
Life threw at us as if we cower
Under its feet.
Still,
We rose from the bird cages.

Soaring above the high waters

Of despair,

Our bond never sunk to the bottom.

Even though our wealth

Isn't calculated to our favor.

Momma always say,

We are rich with dreams and hopes

Of a new day.

In my heart,

Momma is the key to my dreams.

She taught me to be an engine

To my ambitions,

And push with my success.

I want to give momma the world.

For now,

Just in bit and pieces

Until SHE becomes whole.

Cherish

You will never know true happiness

Until you sever the ties of toxic anchors.

Sometimes,

Breathing and smelling the flowers

Brings more joy than putting dreams

Up for collator in a faulty world.

Autopsy

No one will know the true person behind the art.

Until the blood is extracted from the pen,

And the paper is examined.

Antione Denzel Lacey

Sunday Mornings

The odor of stale religion
Filtered the air with the chiming
Sounds of dishes.

Beast stormed through the doors,
Trying to claim a spot
In uncleanse wooden seats.

Snaring with gluttonous grins,
They feasted on the slop
 From hell's kitchen.

They sit and eat.
They stand and watch,
Waiting to devour our ears
With meaningless conversation.

Murderous screams
Echoes through the dining rooms.
We are out of silverware!
Damn…

Forever, We Bloom

Intertwined by our distant hearts

We stand hand and hand.

Pulling the veil

Off for a future generation,

To create and blossom.

We bloom.

Our minds,

Like a garden of flowers.

We watch the sun peak

Over a distant horizon,

Blessing the souls of humanity.

We bloom.

Positive vibes

Consumed in love,

Spreading like a wildfire amongst the youth.

Painting pictures of harmony and greatness, Too.

Forever, we bloom.

Second Line

As the bass shook bones
And moved hushed feet,
It kept the trumpets in line.

Men grabbed their women,
Women grabbed their men,
Interlacing their souls to the dance floor.

The jazzy bass roared over the crowd,
Seducing all flappers alike.
With a girly tune,
Skirts lifted like bottles of old scotch,
To the lips of the drunks.

Trombones tap danced onto the ears
Of the dead,
Hiding cries of laughter.
A celebration of life
Was the motive of the night.

Blood Bond

The doctors said,

I possess the eyes of my mother.

The ability to see hell

And hallucinations all in one.

A broken reality,

Mentally destroyed by the demons

Residing in my head.

Prescription meds isn't the antidote

To cure an infectious trait.

Only to preside silence,

Until the demons

Wake again.

We treat it as normal

As days multiplied by years,

We see it as love.

Another string,

Strengthening the bond

between mother and son.

The optimistic eyes

Don't know a mother's love...

Unless,

She washes her child

With her own sacrificial blood.

Becoming the salvation,

To her child's nightmares.

Our bond is thick,

But our madness runs thin.

Thin enough to slip

Through the cracks of social anxiety.

Realizing,

This not a place for us.

A place where,

The abnormal can't

Be themselves.

This psychological burden

Can inflict rejection

upon the not knowing.

Many will run,

Some will fear.

Not knowing,

What *love* really is.

Focus

Missed what was present
In a dream.
Prayed for it,
To appear in reality.
Desiring the physical need
Of the heart.

Drown

For a long time,

I allowed the deposition of life

To cloud my judgement.

I swung the pendulum,

Between my self-worth and gluttony.

I glorified my pain,

Appetizing it with pleasure.

Thought if I slow danced with death,

I would escape my reality.

The emptiness only left me lonesome,

In the four corners,

Of my existence.

I fell from grace

When a bottle

Of *her*

Hit my lips.

I accepted my darkness,

To see the dim light.

Hang Over

Drink within your thoughts.

The voices become more silent.

Antione Denzel Lacey

Anxiety

The second form of death,
Next to sleep.
The barbwire nooses
Around my neck.
With the hot sensation,
Upon my face.

It creeps itself
Into the nature of my thoughts.
When I run,
It follows.
It enjoys the chase,
My body can't endure.

Anxiety is the shadows,
Of pale darkness,
Lingering in the distance.

Asked if I have prayed,
When anxiety preys on my soul.
Patiently waiting
For me to fail.
It will devour me whole
Like a homemade meal.

Crow's Dream

In my dreams,
I see delusions of my soul
Being vanquished
From my mortal self.

I looked into the distance
And see my salvation.
Only to find a blurry vision.

My view,
The teary eyes of discomfort
And displeasure.
If they only knew,
I mentally release.

Mentally cut the flesh
Of my temple
To rebuild my walls,
And restore my faith.

Funeral

Everyone loves you,

When the flowers bloom.

They'll parade

Upon the victimized eulogies,

Of petals.

Failed to realize,

These flowers die, too.

Wilting away,

With unsaid goodbyes and apologies.

Journey

I walk in the light of God.

My shadows became the demons that followed me.

Antione Denzel Lacey

Untitled

When asked,

Do you believe?

I say "yes" without hesitation.

But,

Religion is a mouth full

And the tables are empty

Within this house.

Letter to My Past

Dear Past,

If these words cannot express the pain

You put me through,

Or the hell only a sinful serpent can endure.

I forgive you.

I understand that shit happens.

I understand tomorrow isn't promised,

And today only fosters hatred.

I understand the earth and the moon

Won't ever touch,

Like the reality, you placed me in.

Nevermore,

I can't hate you.

Hating you only creates another void.

Deeper than the depths of my soul.

This void seems to be no brighter

Than dim street lights on broken fixers.

I tried to burry you

Behind these metaphors and stanzas.

You will always resurrect.

Presenting yourself in the shape

Of Jack Daniels.

In the shape of vodka.

In the shape of some shit, I can't pronounce.

Drowning me in a puddle

Of my own shame.

I brushed it off until the next day,

But the next day is today.

This is not an invitation for you

To stay.

This is not a friendly "hello,"

It is a graceful "goodbye."

Goodbye forever.

Forever as the outcast

In my life.

I won't ever forget the lessons

Presented to me,

Because *you are the never*

That *never* happened.

Be back Soon

He left God to find his Destiny.

Not knowing she was with God waiting for him.

Antione Denzel Lacey

Just Go To Sleep

I call my madness insomnia.

Whenever I want peace

Of mind,

She becomes my headache.

She urges me to write out my dreams

In tax brackets.

Headless,

Like my pillow tossed

Back in a fighting match.

I throw in my dissatisfying towel.

My body rolls itself back over,

To an *unwelcoming* morning.

Steps

Just breathe,

It's okay.

You're not there *yet*.

Trying to fix distorted wounds,

With old bandages.

You've sanitized emotional scrapes

With dried up tears.

The apologies you give yourself

Are more lacerations around

Your neck.

Why are you hurting yourself?

Antione Denzel Lacey

Open Book

If you want to know
My deepest thoughts.
Don't be afraid to venture
Through my pandora box.
Revealing the seal
Of complex uncertainty.

Self-Care

I chose me.

This body cannot move without a mind.

This mind has been under the rubble

Of self-doubt,

Punishing itself through past mistakes.

I wrap my self-love in Bandages,

Asking Mother Time to heal any inflections

To this fragile heart.

I AM MORE…

Repetition

Say my name backwards

Until you regurgitate the meaning

Of a true survivor.

Come to the River

Baptize me in art.

Resurrect me as a masterpiece.

Lost and Found

I lost myself trying to remember

What makes me "*me*."

I walked down lonesome hallways,

Driving to endless destinations

With anxiety in my gas tank.

I tried to find "*me*" through the fumes

Of ganja in the air.

My depression is riding shot gun.

It clutches the wheel,

Every time I swerved.

Until my mind regained focus.

God hitched a ride,

Before my self-destruction.

Ritual

Sage illuminates my room.

Light dances through the windows,

Of my mind.

I hum the sounds of my heart beat.

I've shed away my exoskeleton.

Old bandages,

Applied a new suit to my skin.

I grind the bones,

Smoked the ashes,

Blowing my fears away.

My self-confidence on loud

And my happiness is saying

"Pass that shit."

Antione Denzel Lacey

Note to Self

Don't sacrifice your self-worth,
Paying bills with plantation wages.

Destination

My heart yearns for a place,
I haven't met yet.
A place where the sunsets
Behind the mountains,
And the moon kisses
A blissful horizon.

Immortal

I,

The color black bleed

Not blood,

But ink through my skin.

I engrave the names

Of my lovers.

So,

They won't be forgotten.

I cling onto their memories,

Like treasure.

This becomes longevity,

When another leaves my side.

I,

Am not perfect.

My name gets conversed

Into a song.

As a hormonic lullaby,

Or a hate speech.

I won't ever stay buried.

I rise like pyramids,

Setting over the desert sands

And mountain tops.

Lady Behind the Shades

Her name is unknown.

It is only whispered upon the waters

Of the Mississippi.

She possesses shades,

Which hide the broken windows of her reality.

Criminalized street corners are her playground.

She catches casualties like fireflies illuminated

by the street lights,

trapped in her Venus.

She,

The Charlotte's web to their misery.

If people witnessed her Pandora's box,

She will be shamed in the streets of Babylon.

As if they didn't bear the sins

Of a pretender in the holy house

Of God himself.

She,

The lady who was forced into a cocoon.

Masking her flaws and concealing her pain,

Behind the obscene attire of a saint.

She Said

She said,

If she could be a flower

It would be a daisy.

A daisy flowing freely

In the wind beneath her.

Roses tarnished the hands

Of her lovers.

Other flowers

Aren't as vibrant as her.

She said,

She had seen something

Within myself,

Others could not see.

She had seen the kindness of

A gentleman she hasn't

Seen in many.

I saw a glimpse of heaven,

When I looked into her eyes.

I've seen the passion in her heart,

But if only people could see

The beauty within her soul,

Her golden body

Wouldn't be judged.

Over looked

Like roadside flowers.

The mortal men in her life,

Pulling apart her petals

Leaving her to wither away

And die.

If I could,

I would cradle her

In rejuvenated pot soil.

Knowing this,

Would only be another cage

She tries to escape.

The prisoner within

Her own temple.

Like a phoenix to rise,

Only drowning

In her self-pity.

Rising again,

Only temporarily restored.

She said,

If time prevails,

And this body is no more.

I must remember her

As the daisy.

Remember her as the flower,

Who caressed the lips

of the sun,

And brighten the smiles of all.

She

She is the comparison of me.
Leave her and I in a room alone
And she will take advantage.

Intertwined in armlock,
She exploits my soul.
Fusing her memories with mines
So,
Every moment is cherished.

She is special.
She is the scent of home.
The aphrodisiac of a place
I want to remember.

She gives me hope.
The light to my darkness
And the antidote to my nightmares.
Without her,
She is lost without me.

Antione Denzel Lacey

Beauty with No Name

I look into your eyes,

And see a horizon,

Fit for a king and queen.

Your arms,

The anchors,

keeping me ground between

Reality and my thoughts.

You've embraced me,

With the warm nectar,

Of your lips.

I would ask for your name,

But your beauty is a mystery,

Within itself.

I'll always see you

Tip toeing through my dreams,

Sitting at the edge of my bed.

Waiting for me,

To inhale your presence

And exhale your grace.

Crush

In my prayers,

I see your beautiful face.

I would ask to be yours,

But, my voice was full of fear.

Shamed by my shyness,

I hid behind my mask of discomfort,

Not telling you how I felt.

I couldn't deny your smile.

Your voice is

The harmonic siren

Which kept me at bay.

Waiting to *crash* my ship

Into your rocks -

To hear you speak again.

Antione Denzel Lacey

Ebony

They were afraid of your beauty
In the light.
Now, it dwells within the bosom
Of the shadows.

Bliss

I like a woman,

With the scent of coco butter,

Draped in the conceptions,

Of harmonic blackness.

Her hands,

Balled fist clutching,

Justice in one hand,

And power in the other.

She walks like wind,

Graceful and undistributed.

Amethyst dangles from her,

Crown onto her chest.

She lights sage to mediate.

It burns with her glow,

And cleanses her aura.

Black joy

We kiss the moonlight

And dance without judgement.

Our smiles become the sunrise,

Creating a new morning.

Hardships

Won't define our happiness.

Instead,

It *ignites* the fire

In our bellies

And the motivation

To our wings.

We levitate,

Playing double-dutch

On God's mattress.

Melanin Monroe

Excuse me queen,

Pick yourself up and fix your crown.

The ground is not where you need to be,

Nor kneeling upon the surface

Of mistreatment.

Excuse me queen,

Look into the reflection of beauty,

And realize you're beautiful.

You won't need a justification of proof

When you're looking right at it.

You're not them,

They are not you.

Beauty is in the eyes of the honest,

And truly you are beautiful.

Excuse me queen,

Never bite your tongue.

Bitten words can't speak truth

When the opposition reveals its fangs.

Your words,

The extension of your temple

Breathing life into existence.

It will quiver the fearful nature,

Of any who utter your name.

Stimulations

I want to know you.

I want to know if your thoughts,

Are like my thoughts.

Then,

Our thoughts can create a manifestation

Of a rooted foundation.

Penetration is an art of the seeker,

Seeking entry.

I only seek entry through your mind,

Until your pink prism explodes into

A beautiful super nova of constellations.

Naming every cluster after our son or daughter,

This is just me thinking about a future.

Hide and Seek

Show me your darkness.

I will show you a heart,

Looking for another place to hide.

Morning Talks

We dread the morning,

Peeking through our window

With the bottomless sun.

Twizzlers,

Our fingers

And legs wrapped up,

In covers.

We Inhale each other's scent,

And exhale our moans.

Our bodies quiver,

With the ambitions,

Of finishing each other off.

I,

The oceanic Poseidon,

Venturing through your waters,

In search for Aphrodite's pearl,

In your pink palace.

You,

Released your Nile

And drowned my serpent

In passion.

America

I watched her weep.
The oppressor stripped,
The nature of her skin,
Undressing her culture.

I wanted to run.
I wanted to run and rescue her
From the night terrors,
But,
My body was chained with fear.

Her sadden lullaby voice,
The African sorrow vanishing,
From her crimson body.

She…
Was no more.
Only a hallow shell
Of our ancestors who took her place.
Pain
And suffering were the madness
Spilled onto the floor.

Modern Day Sam

I too am Sam.
I work within the wool of society's underbelly.
My talents display themselves in vibrant
Colors,
But some can only see **one**.

Pushing me into a pile of singularity,
Veiled my pigment behind
My manners.
Synthesizing my spoken language
To all lives matter.

A couple reminded me,
I'm not like the "**others.**"
The "**beauty of darker complexion**" others.
The "**well-spoken,**
But talk with a slur" others.
The "**refusing to go to school,**
Because they're tired of society's bullshit"
Others.

Their monstrous eyes looked at me as though
My fifty shades of brown can be
Diluted into fifty shades of white.

Belittled my ethnicity
With compliments and the back wash
Of make America great again stories.

Fingers like knives upon my melanin,
Obstructing the autopsy of my skin.
They tried to find out what makes me different.
The validation of coco butter running skin deep,
As if *"we"* all smell alike.

Thought a simple smile
Would justify their actions.
Only the anger of my ancestors
Oozed out
Through my metal braces.

The ignorance of their glass house,
Could've been shattered with one word.
Instead,
My God held me
To say "good-bye."

The foolish waddled off
Into the land of nothingness
With their drunken words.

Torn Letter From the Rose Gardener

I forgotten how to breathe.

The word "**can't**" infuse its way

Into my vocabulary,

Every syllable felt like a tighter

Noose around my neck.

Electronic eyes watched my crucifixion.

My lungs collapsed with empathy

For justice,

While my martyr took its last smoke.

I asked for this body

Not to be touched.

My body not be moved,

My body is to be still without judgement.

If me verbalizing my fear

Was wrong,

I asked God why I must becom

Another fruit.

Ripen,

To fall and be hung under the tree... (page torn)

News flash

What do you say,

To a mother who've lost her son?

Nothing,

Because the bullets have already,

Spoken for themselves.

Like text messages,

Holding conversations,

Until the heart leaves the mind,

On "*read*,"

Then *silence*.

God knows we don't need

Another unjustified body

When justice isn't given,

But *silence*.

Silence,

Like the quiet whisper in church,

Muted by grandma's facial expression,

"I will beat that ass."

Silence.

Silence,
Like color coding
Your music in an uncultured
Neighborhood.
Silence.

It only falls on those,
Who ignored it.
Many
Looked away as his body perished.

Rotting for answers on why?
Why this happened to him.
Do you not know a mother's pain?
A father's grief?

Tombstone engraved with his name,
Rest in peace.
But, peace wasn't given.
Instead,
It was taken away
When he was placed in the hearse.

Heroes

My *heroes*,

Don't flaunt their masculinity,

Behind silver bullets.

Their names are engraved,

In the snaps and pops,

of whips and chains.

My *heroes*,

Don't waved their femininity

In the air to show

Their pussies as a Nobel prize.

Instead,

They create majestic heavens

With their words

And bring unchained souls

To the promise land.

My *heroes*,

Aren't found in comics

Or fabricated movies.

My heroes,

Reside in torn freedom papers -

And the obituary pages.

Don't

Don't dismiss **us**.

Weaponized bodies,

Written off with a pen.

Our stories have been gentrified,

And sold on auction.

Falsified names,

In place of our own.

Kunta is here,

And Toby has left the building.

Don't say dismantling my body

Is the justification for you,

Fearing for your life.

No weapons were formed,

But, those unholy bullets prospered.

It wasn't a gun.

You didn't have a right

To unload,

Clips on black bodies

Manifested into a murder's art project.

Don't demonize our culture.

You drank your first baptism

When you turned our blood

Into wine.

Our bodies,

Were the sacrificial lamb,

You pulled from.

ABOUT THE AUTHOR

I describe my poetry as being an "abstract story" filled with things
I want the readers to see and feel while reading my poems.
Whenever I write a poem, I leave a piece of myself inside of the
stanzas or metaphors to make each piece more powerful as my
words give them life. I write poetry to put my mind at ease and
express my art with my pen.

www.ingramcontent.com/pod-product-compliance
Lightning Source LLC
Chambersburg PA
CBHW031934080426
42734CB00007B/684